Hermann Broch

by THEODORE ZIOLKOWSKI

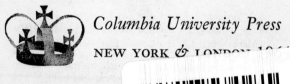

Columbia University Press

NEW YORK & LONDON 1964

COLUMBIA ESSAYS ON MODERN WRITERS is a series of critical studies of English, Continental, and other writers whose works are of contemporary artistic and intellectual significance.

Editor: William York Tindall

Advisory Editors

Jacques Barzun   W.T.H. Jackson   Joseph A. Mazzeo

Hermann Broch is Number 3 of the series.

THEODORE ZIOLKOWSKI is Professor of German Literature at Princeton University. He is author of the forthcoming study, *The Novels of Hermann Hesse.*

103209

Passages from the published works of Broch are quoted, in the author's own translation, from the edition of Broch's works published by Rhein-Verlag, Zürich; passages from unpublished manuscripts are quoted by permission of Yale University Library.

Hermann Broch

Industrialist and poet, mathematician and mystic, rationalist and irrationalist—these are the points of Hermann Broch's emotional compass. His attempt to chart them successively in philosophy, literature, and political action constitutes the basic impulse of his life. Distinguishing between the main trends of contemporary thought, he referred to the position of the positivists as *cogito ergo sum* and that of more existentially oriented thinkers as *sum ergo cogito*. For himself, he concluded, the most satisfactory formulation was *cogito et sum*, with the emphasis on the synthesizing conjunction.

Broch longed for totality and simultaneity—the two words that occur most frequently in his writing. He wanted to encompass all of life—and all at once. This accounts for his literary gigantism, that Gargantua touch inflating everything he undertook to elephantine proportions. It also explains a novel like *The Sleepwalkers*, which sprawls over a period of thirty years, ranging in style from pure lyricism to the abstraction of the essay. It produced finally the monster sentences, textured with *but*, *nevertheless*, *yet*, and *so*, that soar—or lumber, as the case may be—over pages on end. Broch not only wanted to get everything in; it was his aim to bring about a stylistic synthesis of the most disparate elements of being and thought. At his worst, Broch is ponderous, humorless, pedantic, and presumptuous. At his best, he opens up unplumbed areas of literary experience in a manner worthy of his literary idols, Joyce and Kafka.

Broch never romanticized the details of his life. He said that he had at least one thing in common with Franz Kafka and Robert Musil. "We all three have no real biography. We lived and wrote, and that's all." This is not much of an exaggeration. Apart from a few symbolic turning points in his career, Broch's life was one of the mind—a fact highlighted by the impoverished, almost ascetic existence that he led during his last twenty years. At the age of sixty-two he welcomed a ten-month stay in the hospital because it gave him more time to devote to his intellectual work. Yet Broch was no escapist. "The ivory tower is immoral," he said. During his lifetime he saw his share of reality: industrial life in Europe and America before World War I; labor disputes and unemployment in the twenties; Hitler's prisons in the thirties; and the impoverished immigrant's-eye view of New York in the forties.

Born in Vienna in 1886, Broch belonged to the brilliant constellation of apocalyptic poets and writers who chronicled the decline of European civilization as it manifested itself in the Austro-Hungarian Empire at the end of the nineteenth century: Kafka, Musil, Rilke, Georg Trakl, and other stars of a lesser order. Though he was twelve years younger than Hugo von Hofmannsthal, Broch came to realize that they emerged from a similar background, and his study "Hofmannsthal and His Time" assumed the proportions of a symbolic autobiography. This generation of writers devoted themselves to the analysis of a society grown sick and to the search for new values to replace the old. Thus the vision of Broch's dying Vergil is related to the revelations of Rilke's *Duino Elegies*. His *Innocents* are first cousins of Musil's *Man without Qualities*. And his *Sleepwalkers* wander through an often Kafkaesque landscape.

Unlike the others, however, Broch was not a professional

writer. When his first novel appeared in 1931, Hofmannsthal, Rilke, Trakl, and Kafka were dead; Musil had been writing for more than twenty-five years. Meanwhile, Broch had become, as he later said cynically, a captain of industry. As the older son of a Jewish textile manufacturer, Broch was expected to enter the family business. After secondary school he attended lectures on philosophy and mathematics at the University of Vienna, but as a dutiful son his first obligation was to his training at the Technical Institute. This was augmented by practical experience at the Textile School in Mülhausen (Alsace-Lorraine) as well as a journey to the United States in 1906, where he observed milling procedures in the South.

In 1908, after military service as a volunteer officer's candidate in Zagreb, Broch settled down to work in the Teesdorf Mills outside Vienna. As early as 1907 he had taken out patents for a new cotton-mixing appliance and process. By 1915, when his father retired, he was ready to assume the management of the whole concern. For the next ten years he could indeed be called a captain of industry. In addition to supervising the mills, he directed a local military hospital—an experience that provided background for his first novel—served on government advisory councils, and acquired the reputation of a skillful mediator in labor disputes.

It would be wrong to imagine, however, that it was all work and no play. Evenings, after having read a chapter or two of Kant's *Critique of Pure Reason* to his son (who was born in 1910), Broch would sit down at his desk to continue his studies. From 1915 to 1921 he attended courses in mathematics, physics, and logic at the University of Vienna. The immediate result was a series of essays and philosophically oriented literary reviews published between 1913 and 1922 in the liberal Catholic journals *Der Brenner* and *Summa*. Even before his marriage to Franziska von Rothermann in 1909, Broch had become a convert, but the Catholic element in his work is not strong; toward the end of his life he made a conscious effort to "expurgate the remnants of Catholicism" from his thinking. He was attracted to these journals, rather, because *Der Brenner* (in which Trakl's poetry originally appeared) featured the brilliant satirical moralist Karl Kraus, whose work Broch greatly admired, and because *Summa* followed a stated policy of ethical reconstruction on a cosmopolitan level. In these articles and in unpublished studies from 1922 to 1927 Broch developed the theory of values and philosophy of history upon which his literary works depend—indeed, from which the novels directly emerged.

Broch asked himself the question that has concerned historians for generations: How is it possible to determine the essential reality of a given historical period? He begins by reducing the entire problem to one of ethics. Any phenomenon, he maintains, can be explained ultimately by the values of the epoch. In periods of cultural unity, as at the height of the Middle Ages, this is a simple matter. All human activity can be judged as good or bad, right or wrong, by reference to the Christian values handed down by God and interpreted by the Church. The individual is confronted with no ethical decisions and suffers no moral crises because life is regulated by one central authority. But Broch sees history as a dialectic process of two-thousand-year cycles—and here Hegel comes in. Our present cycle—the Christian Era—emerged two thousand years ago from the ruins of the declining pagan era. Developing organically, it reached its apogee in the Middle Ages, and then, at the beginning of modern times, became hypertrophied. "That criminal and rebellious time called the Renaissance, that time in which the Christian system of values was split into a Catholic and a Protestant half" brought about "the process of the five hundred year dissolution of values." In place of the former total system there emerged gradually many partial systems of value. To illustrate this pluralism Broch cites such commonplaces as "business is business," "war is war," and *"l'art pour l'art."*

Contemporary man, living at the end of a historical cycle, is caught between an old system of values that is no longer adequate and a future one that has not yet crystallized. The dilemma of "no longer and not yet"—a key phrase in Broch's vocabulary—is the object of his interest. At this point Broch's speculations begin to merge with those of other contemporary thinkers, for modern man is faced with an essentially existential problem. The "partial systems" are secular ones; thus the man who lives according to the maxim "business is business" has no recourse to a supreme authority if he encounters a situation that does not fit into his narrow framework. If he is not committed to any single partial system, then his dilemma is complicated by the necessity of making empirical choices between systems often in conflict. The result of this pluralism, when the fragile security of the partial system has collapsed, is chaos and despair. Broch sees two possibilities of behavior. A man can attempt to escape the anguish of the present by forgetting himself in the delirium of erotic love or by clinging to the mystical tenets of religious sectarianism. This leads to ethical guilt because it is a flight from reality and responsibility. Or one can take upon oneself the burden of freedom by disavowing the facile solutions of partial systems and attempting to make "realistic" decisions. This means alienation and loneliness since freedom is a road chosen by few; but it prepares the way for the future and a new system of values by sweeping away the residue of the past.

Broch's dialectic process has pushed God right out of the picture. He is concerned, like Kant, with finding what he calls "the Earthly Absolute"—ethical values postulated solely on the fact of man's existence. He never denies the existence of the transcendental, however. As a matter of fact, it plays a major role in his thought, for part of the total synthesis of opposites that Broch hopes to achieve in his *unio mystica* is the reconciliation of life and death, the here and the beyond, the present and the future. For this reason, symbols have an important function. We cannot know what is transcendental; but things and actions on earth can "echo" or "mirror" the divine. In this, as in many other respects, Broch is close to Romantic poets like Novalis, who regarded natural phenomena as hieroglyphs, or *chiffres*, of the transcendental. And precisely this "romantic" aspect of his work links him with German contemporaries like Hermann Hesse and Thomas Mann while distinguishing him from other existential authors with whom he has much in common. However, man must create his ethical values as though there were nothing outside this world. Here Broch reaches a solution that is close to Camus's concept of human dignity and solidarity. Later, in his Theory of Humane Politics, Broch developed this idea into a more elaborate system. But at this point his ethical postulate is summed up best by the Biblical quotation that closes *The Sleepwalkers:* "Do thyself no harm: for we are all here" (Acts 16:28).

One might well ask why Broch found it necessary to put all of this into fictional form. The decision—indeed, the necessity—can be explained by his intellectual crisis of 1928. That year Broch shocked his family by selling the mills in order to return to the University of Vienna, where he planned to obtain a doctorate in philosophy and mathematics. There were certain practical motivations. Broch sensed that an economic crisis was approaching and felt that his move was financially sound. But we would be cheap to doubt the sincerity of his motives. As a man whose whole life was devoted to "cognition," he had reached a point in his philosophical work from which he could not go on without further study and total commitment. Fortunately for literature, Broch went back to the University just at a time when absolutes were becoming unfashionable. In philosophy the logical positivists had discarded metaphysical speculation in favor of problems that could be solved by mathematical demonstration. As Broch wrote, Wittgenstein and his followers regarded ethics as "unscientific" and "mystical." (Broch himself had studied with Carnapp, Hahn, Menger, and others.) For Broch this realization was unsettling.

I discovered something else: those areas of philosophy that are inaccessible to mathematical treatment—primarily ethics or metaphysics—become "objective" only in the realm of theology. Otherwise they become relativistic and, ultimately, "subjective." It was this subjectivity that forced me into the area where it is radically legitimate, namely into literature.

Broch's language is ponderous, but the meaning is clear. Ethical absolutes are possible only within a theological system. But our theological system—Christianity—has disintegrated, as Broch had concluded from his philosophy of history. If ethical postulates outside of theology are by definition relative or subjective, then one should deal with them in a form that is frankly subjective—in literature.

Within a year of returning to the University Broch gave up his plans for a doctorate and undertook his first novel. This reaction repeated itself several times during his life when he found it necessary to turn to literature in order to express ideas that are not the legitimate concern of philosophy. For this reason—and with some justification—Broch has been called "a writer *malgré lui*." He certainly never wrote a novel simply to satisfy an aesthetic impulse. He even coined the expression "epistemological novel" to designate his works. But this must not blind us to the fact that Broch, even if he reached literature by the back door, was a born writer. When he allows himself to succumb to "the temptation to tell stories," he is

[9]

capable of writing with a creative surge matched by few of his contemporaries. When his works sag, it is because he has tried to load them down with too heavy a burden of unassimilated speculation.

For Broch, then, literature is an epistemological short cut—what he sometimes called "an impatience for cognition." In a "methodological prospectus" of his first novel that he wrote for his publisher he explained:

This novel is based on the assumption that literature must concern itself with those human problems that are rejected by science because they are not open to rational treatment . . . and with those problems whose solution science, in its slower and more precise progress, has not yet reached. The area of literature between the "no longer" and "not yet" of science has thus become more limited, but also more secure; it encompasses the whole realm of irrational experience, specifically in the border-area where the irrational manifests itself as deed, thus becoming expressible and representable.

This conception of the proper realm of literature supplied the title for his novel. "Sleepwalkers" are individuals existing in a state of suspension between two ethical systems or two cycles of reality—just as the sleepwalker lives between sleeping and waking, partaking of both. Broch's sleepwalkers are no longer satisfied by the ethical codes of the past, yet they cannot free themselves completely. In his novels Broch is concerned always with the critical *Grenzsituationen* (border situations) in which a man's accepted standards are shown to be deficient by the intrusion of something irrational—what Broch calls the "irruption from below." Because the behavior of the characters is no longer rational but motivated by vague irrational impulses, the novels take on a dreamlike quality often associated with Kafka's fiction.

The Sleepwalkers (1931–32) belongs to a group of major

German novels that analyzed the disintegration of society culminating in the catastrophe of World War I: *The Man without Qualities*, *The Magic Mountain*, Hermann Hesse's *Demian*, and Joseph Roth's *Radetzky March*. In structure and style, however, it is far more radically experimental than the others. Broch was never a man to shrink from the consequences of consistency; his unwillingness to compromise led him to give up, first, his business career and then his academic pursuits. During the four years he was working on his novel, he read widely and eagerly exploited any techniques that seemed expedient for his own purposes. The result is a work that shows the clear influence of such diverse authors as John Dos Passos, André Gide, James Joyce, Franz Kafka, and Aldous Huxley and yet manages to attain an astonishing degree of artistic integration.

"The age of the polyhistorical novel has dawned," he announced to his publisher. (For his faith, patience, and advice Dr. Daniel Brody of the Rhein-Verlag should take his place in the annals of publishing beside Thomas Wolfe's editor, Maxwell Perkins.) Broch had noted the polymath tendencies of Mann, Musil, Huxley, and other contemporaries. Most writers, he observed, regarded their erudition as "a block of crystal" from which they chipped off scintillating bits to insert into their stories in the form of "cultivated" conversations. Like them, Broch hoped to achieve "polyhistorical" totality, but he did not want to slacken the tension of the narrative. Nor did he want, at the other extreme, to interrupt the action for the subjective ruminations of the author. Why not be absolutely consistent? He came up with the idea of separating these functions of the rational and the irrational completely—by including seventeen chapters of pure lyricism as a vehicle for the subjective voice of the narrator and ten chapters of an essay entitled "The Disintegration of Values," which comprises

[11]

roughly the ideas on theory of values and philosophy of history developed during the twenties. Between these two extremes the action is suspended.

The novel is a trilogy. *Pasenow the Romantic* takes place in the year 1888 in Berlin and the province of Brandenburg and centers on members of the Prussian nobility. *Esch the Anarchist* moves to the urban working class of Cologne and Mannheim in 1903. *Huguenau the Realist*, finally, is localized in the bourgeois society of a small village on the Mosel in the months preceding the November Revolution of 1918. Even this external organization reveals the symbolic structure. Just as the sequence in time traces the emergence of a new "objective" man from the romanticism and anarchy of the past, so too the movement from east to west signifies a progression from eastern mysticism toward western rationalism—a geographical symbolism that would not be lost on Thomas Mann, who was fond of playing with similar conceits.

This development is reflected in the style of the parts. *Pasenow* is written in such a subtle parody of late nineteenth-century realism that the incautious reader might take the novel to be a period piece from the pen of Theodor Fontane—a comparison that many contemporary critics made. Only careful attention to Broch's use of point of view reveals that the narrator has carefully excluded himself from the story; every incident is consistently related in its filtration through various shifting focuses. "Reality" turns out to be anything but the stable world of traditional realism, and its breakdown is anticipated stylistically. In Part Two this collapse is overt. There is no longer even the exterior semblance of order, and this chaos is reflected in the hectic expressionistic prose that can rise, on demand, to a high pitch of lyricism. In the third volume the structure corresponds to the complete disintegration of reality. There is no homogeneity of style; instead, lyric, dramatic, narrative, expository, and reportorial elements occur independently in separate chapters. The analytic disintegration of style mirrors the objective attitude of the hero toward reality.

Within this framework Broch tells the story of four representative individuals. Joachim von Pasenow is a "romantic" because he clings desperately to values that virtually everyone else regards as outmoded. His "emotional lethargy" (*Trägheit des Gefühls*) lends to his character a certain old-fashioned quaintness, but it renders him almost totally unfit to deal with any situation that does not fit into his narrow code, whose romantic values are symbolized by his lieutenant's uniform. Whenever he is confronted by a perplexing situation, he nervously fingers the buttons to make sure that he is properly enclosed and insulated against outside forces. It represents the gravest threat to his existence to be "dragged down" into civilian life, where his military code is not valid, where he is not protected by his uniform. The threat of irrationalism, the "irruption from below," comes in the form of love. Pasenow's code has no place for a purely human relationship; in his mind, love is either degraded to pure eros, as in his affair with the barmaid Ruzena, or it is sublimated into a quasi-religious experience. His complete incompetence in dealing with the reality of love is the point of the novel. The story ends on his wedding night, when Joachim is rendered temporarily impotent by his inability to treat Elisabeth as a woman instead of a symbol of the divine. Our last glimpse shows Joachim lying fully dressed beside his new bride, nervously straightening his jacket when it falls open and reveals his black trousers. (In the symbol-laden book the color black stands for the dark recesses of erotic desire.)

Pasenow sets the pattern for the following volumes. In all three we are shown a thirty-year-old man whose system of

[13]

values is threatened for the first time by irrationality. (This is, by the way, the pattern in Kafka's *Trial* as well as in Thomas Mann's stories "Little Herr Friedemann" and "The Clown.") Pasenow's reaction to the "irruption from below" is a desperate, "romantic" clinging to the past. August Esch, at loose among the "anarchic" pluralism of the present, lives by the down-to-earth motto "business is business." As an accountant he views the whole world in terms of bookkeeping. Until his thirtieth year this conception was quite adequate; nothing made him question the debits and credits of life. Then, without warning, he is fired from his job. Esch knows that he has made no mistake in his books. He was dismissed in order to cover up the embezzlement of a superior. He has been punished for another man's guilt. This realization upsets Esch's whole cosmic account book. Instead of going to the police, Esch makes the mistake of blackmailing the embezzler for a good recommendation to another position. By trying not to become involved, he complicates the situation. The debit of guilt must be offset by the credit of expiation in order to keep the books straight. If the perpetrator is not punished, then someone else must suffer. The whole novel, one of Broch's strongest narratives, is moved along by Esch's attempts to reestablish the cosmic harmony. He interprets everything that happens in terms of the initial debt. Thus when he meets Ilona, the partner of a knife-thrower in a burlesque show, he sees her in his confused mind as a symbol of the divine who must suffer crucifixion every night because of the unexpiated guilt in the world. "Without order in the accounts there was also no order in the world, and as long as there was no order, Ilona would continue to be exposed to the knives, Nentwig would continue, insolent and hypocritical, to escape his penance." Esch, like Pasenow, is caught between two women, but can accept neither of them as a person. While Ilona represents the spiritualization of love,

[14]

Mother Hentjen, whom he eventually marries, offers simple forgetfulness in erotic union. In view of the elaborate parallelism of the two volumes it is significant that Pasenow, the romantic, chooses the solution of spiritualization in his marriage to Elisabeth while Esch, in the face of a chaotic world, seeks oblivion in the arms of Mother Hentjen. Both incur guilt by fleeing ethical responsibility.

Eduard von Bertrand is the only figure who connects parts one and two. In the first part he is Pasenow's acquaintance: a former officer who had done the unheard of—given up his uniform for the world of business. In Part Two he has become the owner of the shipping company that employs Esch. Bertrand represents still a third ethical position: the aesthetic one. Conscious, like Pasenow and Esch, of the existence of various sets of values, he tries to stand above them—not bound, but also not yet completely free. He advises Pasenow to rid himself of outworn values and to live freely. Unable to accept the consequences of his own advice, he commits suicide in Part Two, a true victim of the dilemma of "no longer and not yet." He never actually appears in Part Two; we encounter him only in Esch's thoughts and visions.

In all of Broch's novels sex functions as a key symbol of man's response to reality. Pasenow becomes impotent because he is unable to come to terms with love. Esch hurls himself into sexual intercourse with complete abandon in an attempt to forget reality. The sterility of Bertrand's aesthetic position is emphasized by his homosexuality. The only figure who masters sex and thus triumphs over reality is Huguenau, the "hero" of volume three. No repressions, self-abandonment, or deviation for him. He goes to the brothel once a week for hygienic reasons, and when it seems like an expedient thing to do, he rapes Mother Hentjen, Esch's wife.

In this final volume Esch and Pasenow have both ended up in

[15]

the little Mosel village: Pasenow as commandant of the town, and Esch as owner and editor of the local newspaper. Their inability to come to grips with reality brings the two men together in a religious sect, but it is precisely this longing for a vague mystical escape that constitutes their ethical guilt. This spurious harmony is disrupted when Huguenau arrives on the scene. Huguenau's objectivism, his complete break with the past, is symbolized by his desertion from the army. During the six months before the November Revolution he is a totally free or "valueless" man, bound in no way to any standards of the past. (It is, by the way, a position that he is unable to sustain: at the end of the novel he slips back into a handy system of values as soon as the "holiday mood" of the war is over.) Broch does not imply that Huguenau is an admirable man; far from it, many of his actions are contemptible. Yet Broch calls him "my portrait or at least (to use Freud's language) my super-ego" because he represents, during this six-month "vacation" the objective approach to reality that is necessary in order to overcome the useless ideals of the past and take vengeance upon Pasenow and Esch for their ethical guilt. This freewheeling attitude makes it possible for Huguenau to arrive in town, a penniless deserter, and within a short time become one of the leading citizens. He swindles Esch out of his newspaper and bullies Pasenow into submission, so that the commandant will not report him as a deserter. During the revolution he murders Esch, and as a final gesture of contempt for those who adhere to mystical ideals, rapes his wife. When the revolution is over, Pasenow and Esch are dead; the forces of objectivism have won out over the romanticism and anarchy of the past.

Though the three volumes can be read separately, they constitute a connected trilogy in which the strongest links of continuity are leitmotiv and symbol. Pasenow is characterized repeatedly by his "emotional lethargy"; Esch is identified by the "impetuosity" with which he responds to the anarchic world about him; and Bertrand's disengagement is signified by his "deprecatory gesture," which is picked up by Pasenow and Esch and thus occurs in all three volumes. (The English translation does not render these leitmotivs consistently in all three parts.) The symbol of the uniform, which is central in volume one, figures in the other parts, but in a degraded "de-romanticized" form. The customs inspector Korn, who is not perturbed by the reality that Esch finds so disturbing, struts about in the authority of his uniform. The members of the Salvation Army, who find the illusion of stability in their sectarianism, wear a uniform. Conversely, the shattering of reality is signified by the loss of uniform, as in the troubled patients of the military hospital in Part Three. In all three volumes travel is a symbol of escape to freedom. Bertrand's business takes him all over the world, but since he never frees himself completely from the past, he returns to Germany and dies there. In volume two Esch dreams of going to America. When his dream cannot be fulfilled, he buys himself a reproduction of the Statue of Liberty as a symbol of his longing, and in volume three Huguenau notices it, with contempt, on Esch's desk. These, as well as many of the other leitmotivs and symbols that recur through all three volumes, give the trilogy as a whole a consistent texture and contribute to the effect of simultaneity and totality that Broch was anxious to achieve.

In volume three the focus is expanded to embrace more than the Huguenau-Esch-Pasenow plot. To represent the themes of disintegration and alienation, Broch has constructed a series of parallel plots connected, in the manner of Dos Passos, by occasional nodal chapters. At the same time, the various parallel plots are sustained in an inner tension by a counterpoint technique derived from Huxley. In these narrative strands Broch depicts disintegration, for instance, in the person of the shell-shocked veteran Gödicke, who must laboriously reconstruct his personality from the disparate elements that he finds in his consciousness when he comes out of his coma. The spiritual imbalance of the age is personified by the wounded Lieutenant Jaretzki, an architect by profession (that is, a symbol of proportion), who has lost an arm and must now get used to an artificial limb. And the progressive stages of loneliness are shown in the story of Hanna Wendling, who is gradually alienated from her husband while he is at the Eastern Front. These subplots, only tenuously connected with the main action, are all part of Broch's attempt to attain symbolic totality.

At either extreme of these graded narrative sections, the lyrical portions and the discursive essay "The Disintegration of Values" are built into the novel in a delicate counterpoint to the other chapters. At first glance the tale told in the ballad seems even more incongruous than the essay. The essay at least deals overtly with the problems suggested by the narrative, but the lyrical passages tell a completely unrelated story: the love between a girl from the Salvation Army in Berlin and the Jew Nuchem—a love doomed to failure because of irreconcilable differences in religion. We gradually realize, however, that the narrator of the ballad, Dr. Bertrand Müller —perhaps a spiritual heir of Eduard von Bertrand but certainly not physically identical with him—is at the same time the author of "The Disintegration of Values." Since the essay, in turn, embraces the various plots, he is by extension the author of the entire novel.

Now we begin to understand the implications of Broch's decision to give up philosophy in order to write fiction. He found modern philosophy insufficient because it disregarded whole areas of human experience: the irrational, the ethical, the metaphysical. Hence, the "irrational" implications of the essay had to be dealt with as plots or stories showing the actual confrontation of human beings with irrational or ethical decisions; the essay produces the fiction. At the same time, Broch had learned from the theories of modern science that even in the so-called pure sciences cognition is not absolute, but relative. Just as in the physics of Einstein or Heisenberg the phenomenon observed is affected by the position and nature of the observer, so too in the philosophical disciplines every idea is conditioned by the character of the person who thinks it. In order to present an idea, one must at the same time present the personality of the thinker. The subject of observation, as Broch put it, must be projected into the field of observation as an *object* of observation. This was a notion that fascinated Broch, and he discussed its applicability to the works of writers like Joyce and Gide. (The technique that he finally evolved is indebted in no small measure to Gide's *Counterfeiters*, which he greatly admired.) The subjective personality of the writer had to be defined in the lyrical passages in order to justify, as it were, the theoretical essay of the same writer. In the essay and the plots Bertrand Müller is the observing subject; in the ballad he exposes himself as an *object* of observation. What we have, then, is actually an absolute novel that represents the full extent of Bertrand's mind, with its scope from the rational down to the depths of the irrational. The ballad is ultimately the only "subjective" strand of the entire book; as such, it is properly written in the "subjective" mode, namely in lyrical form. Years later, in connection with *The Innocents*, which has a similar lyrical "super-voice," Broch explained: "The only thing that can possibly match the enormous volume of our time is the volume of the I or the Self; and it, in turn, is so large that it cannot be expressed purely in novelistic form, but requires purely lyrical forms." It is this emphasis on the lyrical nature of the subject that distin-

[19]

guishes Broch's work from, say, Thomas Mann's *Doctor Faustus* or *The Holy Sinner*, where the personality of the narrative subject is clearly defined—but in the narrative mode and for purposes of irony rather than in the lyrical mode for reasons of cognition.

Broch had great hopes for his novel. Though it was begun as an epistemological exercise, he was not unaware of its literary merits. Since he saw it as "a *novum* in the form of the novel," he hoped for wide publicity. He was eager for the work to be selected by the Book-of-the-Month Club in the United States and even discussed the possibility of filming it with Warner Brothers. (These were hopelessly unrealistic dreams, but it should be pointed out in Broch's defense that his common sense was outweighed at this time by financial distress.) Broch, having become keenly aware of his position in the world of literature, compared his work with assurance to the novels of Joyce, Mann, Gide, and others. He was particularly pleased when Edwin and Willa Muir undertook the English translation of *The Sleepwalkers*, because they had translated Kafka. And Broch was initially attracted to the Rhein-Verlag, which published his works, because it had brought out the German translation of *Ulysses*.

The complicated relationship of Broch to Joyce can barely be sketched here, but it is exceedingly important. As soon as Broch read *Ulysses*—while he was working on the third draft of his own novel—he was struck by the similarity of intention. "If I had read *Ulysses* before I wrote *The Sleepwalkers*," he said, "my novel would have remained unwritten." He urged his publishers to stress the connection between his book and *Ulysses*. "I agree to any propaganda that couples me with Joyce." In a letter to a friend he called Joyce "my literary super-ego." Yet this adulation must not obscure the true relationship. Joyce's impact on *The Sleepwalkers* is much less than that of Dos Passos, Huxley, and Gide. The only explicit alteration that Broch undertook after he read *Ulysses* was to remove the Odysseus framework that originally introduced and concluded the third volume as an archetypal analogy. Otherwise *The Sleepwalkers* is organized according to entirely different structural principles. Broch contrasted his own "additive" technique—the separation of the rational and the irrational into various parallel strands—with the "synthetic" method of Joyce. He was most impressed by Joyce's awareness of "the mission of literature [to create] a cognition that embraces totality" and by the "inner simultaneity" of *Ulysses*. He felt that Joyce came closer than any other contemporary to fulfilling the requirements of the polyhistorical novel, which he saw foreshadowed in Goethe's late novel *Wilhelm Meister's Travels*. The essay Broch wrote in honor of Joyce's fiftieth birthday is a brilliant interpretation of Joyce's work, but at the same time a statement of Broch's own position. He never accepted Joyce's method wholeheartedly. In his letters and essays Joyce's name occurs dozens of times, but it is always obvious that Broch regards Joyce as a challenge and uses him as a counterfoil for his own thoughts. Though his *Death of Vergil* is much closer to Joyce than *The Sleepwalkers*, he employed in it a technique that he explicitly contrasted with Joyce's "psychoanalytic pointillism." It is impossible to think of Broch without the impact of Joyce. Yet in his approach to literature, as in everything else, Broch vacillated between two poles.

At the other pole stood Franz Kafka. "Art which does not render the totality of the world is not art," Broch wrote again and again. But there are two ways to achieve totality: the complicated way of the "polyhistorical" novel, and the simple way of myth. In the former, Broch felt, Joyce was unexcelled. But mythic literature is of a higher order altogether, and here Kafka was master. "Myth is the archetype of philosophy,"

Broch claimed. "Either poetry is able to proceed to myth or it goes bankrupt." In myth the irrational and rational elements of being are united in one grand vision; there is no need for the analytic methods of the polyhistorical novel and the intellectual gymnastics of the *poeta doctus*. In primitive myth we see a stage of intuitive knowledge of unity before cultural disintegration has set in. And literature, if it is to be worth while, must go forward until it succeeds in establishing a new myth. Kafka, Broch felt, intuitively attained with simple means such mythical validity that he had no need of the "complicated" techniques of Joyce. Broch hoped to achieve something like a synthesis of Joyce and Kafka in what he called the "meta-novel." He formulated "three imperative, yet unrealizable requirements" for the new novel: it must employ total radicality of means; it must strive to attain cognition of death; and it must achieve radicality of myth. These three imperatives are subsumed, Broch concluded, in a fourth and most important one: the "totality-weight" or "totality-gravity" (*Totalitätsgewicht*) of the work of art.

Broch experimented in various directions before, in 1934, he began his second major novel. In addition to writing literary and philosophical essays he contemplated a sequel to *The Sleepwalkers*, which would carry its theme on into the thirties. The only fruit of this activity, beside some fragments, was his play *The Atonement*, performed in 1934. Broch also blocked out elaborate plans for a series of stories revolving around the signs of the zodiac.

The zodiac stories are an experiment. They attempt to make the reader "experience" certain primal symbols of the human soul, such as the lion, the bull, the fish, but also the triangle; that is, to produce an emotional situation from which it becomes self-evident that these images assumed that metaphysical symbolic character that bestows upon a concrete and often trivial object the power of representing a great supersensory realm.

[22]

Although Broch never completed this project, various stories subsequently found a place in *The Innocents*. The plan itself is of interest because it reveals Broch's growing curiosity about the nature of symbols. (The triangle, for instance, becomes a centrally important symbol in *The Innocents* for the emptiness of a hermetically isolated existence.) This fascination with symbols ties in with Broch's theory of the novel as it developed in connection with Joyce and Kafka. "If there is any meaning in art, then it lies principally in being able to express totality with a limited number of motives."

The only longer work during these two years was the novel *The Unknown Quantity*, which Broch wrote in six weeks in 1933. Though unquestionably inferior to the four major novels, it is a symptomatic effort. It resulted from a grandiose scheme that Broch outlined in a lengthy correspondence with Warner Brothers. Broch, like C. P. Snow more recently, tended to regard himself as a mediator between two cultures. He envisaged a series of six motion pictures that would familiarize the general public with the mind of the scientist in order to combat the anti-intellectualism of the times. (It was one of his pet ideas that the film is the only adequate art form for modern society since it is the legitimate product of an industrialized collective society. For similar publicistic reasons he had the novel printed as a newspaper serial.) The project—like most of Broch's ambitious enterprises—got no further than this first novel, which was to be the basis for the scenario. The book is not unlike C. P. Snow's *The Search*, which appeared the following year. The basic pattern is again the "irruption from below" in the life of a young mathematician. The "unknown quantity" of the title, which does not fit into his hyperrational system, comes in the form of a love affair and the death of his brother. Broch was interested in demonstrating that the scientist's reaction to the problems of existence is not different

[23]

from that of the politician, the businessman, or the technologist. The novel is far too hastily and schematically executed to have any literary merit; it is little more than a variation on the theme of *The Sleepwalkers*. But one important ingredient has been added: death as a manifestation of the irrational. Broch's earlier protagonists had to come to terms with love. Richard Hieck learns that life alone does not embrace all experience. "Death and life together constitute the totality of being."

In 1935 Broch left Vienna to live in the Tyrolese village of Mösern near Seefeld. Here, and later in the Styrian Alps around Alt Aussee, he worked on his "mountain novel," *The Bewitchment*. Like Thomas Mann's novel, *The Bewitchment* depicts a "magic mountain"—but instead of rendering in hermetic isolation a model of contemporary civilization, it goes to the other extreme and portrays the mythic origins of human society. Like *The Sleepwalkers*, this novel deals with a critical year in which traditional values are threatened by the intrusion of irrational forces. But Broch is concerned here not with an individual or group of individuals, but with a village as a collective society. It is a study in mass hysteria. The novel relates how the isolated village of Kuppron comes under the spell of the stranger Marius Ratti, who arrives with promises to relieve the destitution of the people. He proposes to open up the ancient gold mines in the nearby mountains and preaches a return to the values of the primitive Celts who originally inhabited the area, persuading the villagers that their troubles stem from the meretricious effects of modern industrialization. He works the villagers up to such a pitch of feverish blindness that they actually render a human sacrifice to the powers of the mountain before their hysteria subsides.

As sheer narrative this is the most impressive of Broch's novels. There is virtually no intrusion of speculative thought;

all the meaning has been assimilated into the action. Yet the work has several important levels of meaning beyond the plot itself: political, psychological, and mythical. In the first place the novel constitutes an analysis of the rise of Nazism. Marius Ratti has personal characteristics borrowed from Hitler: his physical appearance as well as his perverse chastity fit the popular image. He exerts an almost irresistible magnetism upon those who listen to him, and he gathers about him a group of young enthusiasts who are like storm troopers. His political technique depends upon the resuscitation of primitive myth as well as the creation of a scapegoat like the Jews: the Protestant Wetchy, who is both an "outsider" and, as a machine salesman, the representative of industrialization. The corruption of Kuppron corresponds almost step by step to the seduction of Germany in the twenties and thirties.

The specific points that Broch borrowed from contemporary politics correspond to the outline for a "Study of Mass Hysteria" that he submitted in 1942 to the Rockefeller Foundation. Broch's theory of mass psychology, which has many points in common with Sartre's "Portrait of an Anti-Semite," emerged as a consistent extension of his theory of values and philosophy of history. The protagonists of his first novel existed in an intermediate "sleepwalker" state between systems of value; their consciousness was one that Broch defined as "twilight condition" in his mass psychology. "While an isolated individual is prone to accept his being confronted with inexplicable phenomena, the human mind within the 'pre-panicky' mass seeks an 'explicable' cause for the phenomenon, primarily a human one. The alien bearing all marks of the non-ego becomes its very symbol." A fearmonger like Marius exploits these inchoate anxieties, for the mass eagerly follows any leader who promises to relieve its uncertainty. *The Sleep-*

walkers ended with the longing for "a Leader to take him tenderly and lightly by the hand, to set things in order and show him the way." In his mass psychology Broch warns that often a false prophet comes in the guise of the true Leader. Superficially resembling the Leader, he promises instead of a new reality merely a return to an old system of values. For humankind, as T. S. Eliot observed, "cannot bear very much reality." This is how Broch explains the almost mystical appeal of Hitler; and this justifies the function of Marius Ratti in the novel. The escape has a temporary appeal, but its satisfaction cannot last, for the old system ignores too much present reality; in order to support the system, it is necessary to do violence to any inexplicable phenomenon. But eventually reality, asserting itself, ousts the false leader and inaugurates a new era.

On this level the novel presents the paradigm of an eternal mythic process. Following the theories of Bachofen, Broch depicts a society just emerging from the state of matriarchy. The good forces of the village, eventually overcome by Marius and his gang, are represented by Mother Gisson, a modern hypostasis of the *magna mater*. She has found what Broch calls the "knowledge of the heart"—a *unio mystica* of spirit and body, life and death, present and future. Her warnings go unheeded as the villagers respond ever more blindly to the inducements of Marius. Yet she realizes that this hysteria is part of the inevitable historical process, for an antichrist like Marius is needed to sweep away the old order so that a new order can emerge. "My time is up, but it is without end . . . the stranger will wander on and pass away . . . then you will no longer believe in hatred." When the villagers sacrifice a girl to the mountain in order to gain access to the gold, they symbolically reenact a primitive Celtic rite. They do not realize that their sacrifice is actually a travesty and not redemption;

for it is a step back into the strictures of the past rather than an advance into the freedom of the future.

In an English synopsis of the novel that he submitted to the Guggenheim Foundation Broch wrote the following justification:

It is quite within the realm of possibility to give "objective descriptions" of events involving mass psychology. A procession of medieval flagellants, the roar of a foot-ball game, the crowds in front of the Berlin Reich Chancellery listening to Hitler's strange inflections from the balcony, the horrors of a pogrom—all these can be vividly brought to life. But all such depictions—even though they have historical validity—remain empty words. They merely state the facts of certain mass movements, failing to say anything about their true function and effectiveness. For enlightenment on these points one must turn to the mind of the individual; one must ask why and in which manner the individual participates in that incomprehensible mass behavior. How is it possible that man, when under that spell, is prepared to accept the crudest lies as gospel truth; how can a person otherwise prudent and capable of self-criticism, become involved in the most fantastic adventures; why do archaic tendencies believed long buried come to the fore; why do supernatural trends suddenly appear within rational minds? Only the individual who has fallen under the spell can explain.

Here Broch implicitly refers to the political, psychological, and mythical dimensions mentioned above. But the last sentence opens our eyes to still another aspect. This novel also emerged as the answer to a methodological dilemma. In his studies of mass hysteria Broch had gone as far as he could. For the ultimate answers he had to turn to the subjective element, the mind of the individual. The novel is a first-person narrative by the village doctor, who came to Kupprou some ten years earlier in order to escape the chaos of the city and find peace in a union with nature. He witnesses, even participates in, the events of the terrible six months in the village. Then, in the nine months immediately following, he sets down his memories of all that has happened. Ostensibly it is the calm record of an objective observer—one who is "otherwise prudent and capable of self-criticism." What makes the novel a frightening indictment of mass hysteria is the fact that the narrator himself changes without realizing it. At the end he reports that everything has returned to normal. Mother Gisson is dead; Marius Ratti has been absorbed into the village council; life goes on. The doctor himself has been so much caught up in the web of complicity that he does not realize how radically the village has actually changed. The narrator is not trustworthy. Again Broch is playing tricks of relativism on the reader. The narrative subject turns out to be, at the same time, a narrative object. When we reach the end of the novel we gradually realize that we must reevaluate everything we have read in the light of the shifting character of the doctor himself. Things have returned to "normal" in the village only because he himself has come to regard the new situation as normal. In reality a whole cultural epoch has died away and been replaced by a new one.

Although *The Bewitchment* was originally planned as part of a "religious trilogy," Broch never finished even this first volume. Between 1934 and 1936 he wrote two drafts, and in 1950–51 he worked on a third revision. But the published version is a posthumous collation of the three manuscripts. Even the German title (*Der Versucher*) is not Broch's own. (There is no English translation, but Broch referred to the novel in English as "The Bewitchment.") He called it variously his "mountain novel," "Demeter or the Bewitchment," "The Stranger," and "The Wanderer," as in his mind the emphasis shifted from the symbolism of the mountain to the figure of Mother Gisson and to the character of Marius. Yet the novel is complete and represents, next to Thomas Mann's *Doctor Faustus*, the most profound fictional portrayal of the rise of irrationalism in Germany during the Hitler era. The three versions differ generally only in style, acquiring progressively more symbolic density. It was another intellectual crisis that caused Broch, in 1936, to give up a major novel that was so near completion.

While I was writing my mountain novel, I noticed the tendency toward myth—discovered it successively, so to speak—and discovered at the same time the insufficiency of my beginning, so that I simply left the book as it was—especially since it had simply become unbearable for me to disguise this insufficiency in fictional form.

This sentence marks the culmination of an attitude that had been growing in Broch's mind for some time. As early as 1933 we find him asking, in a spirit of curious inquiry, whether literature is a legitimate pursuit. Although he is skeptical enough to pose the question, he finds that there are at least two good answers. First, literature is a short cut to knowledge —what he calls "cognition through form" because it arrives intuitively at results that science and philosophy can reach only through a sequence of tedious preliminary steps. Secondly, it serves, in our secular age, as a surrogate for religion. Gradually, however, his doubts grew stronger. Is not literature, he muses uneasily, an aesthetic escape from reality? Is the writer not simply trying to create in his mind an artificially ordered universe in which it is easier to live than in the world of reality? Ultimately Broch reaches the conclusion that art is immoral, for in its search for beauty it flees ethical responsibility by effacing distinctions between good and evil. If our everyday reality, according to his theory of history, is not in itself real—if we are living in a state of "no longer and not yet" between true cultural epochs—then our literature is really not a reflection of reality (which would be legitimate), but a reflection of a mere *reflection* of reality. In the era of gas chambers, when the ethical imperative is reduced to the simplest mandate of love for one's fellow man, it is "a sacrilege" to seek escape through art. And any attempt to beautify the horror of existence through art is "perjury."

When he had reached this nadir of despair in 1936, Broch was invited to read one of his stories on the Viennese radio. Since he had just renounced literature for reasons of principle, Broch volunteered a talk on "Literature at the End of a Cultural Epoch," in which he proposed to elucidate his doubts concerning the validity of art. For technical reasons the radio network insisted on having a story rather than an essay. With the irony characteristic of his life, Broch was forced to resort to literature in order to express his skepticism about literature. The legend of Vergil, according to which the dying poet wanted to burn his *Aeneid*, suggested itself to Broch as a vehicle for his thoughts. Because of his belief in the two-thousand-year cycle of history Broch was able to regard Vergil, coming between the pagan and Christian eras, as a prototype of the modern man of "no longer and not yet." And the legend implied that Vergil, too, must have entertained similar doubts regarding the legitimacy of literature if he wanted to destroy his lifework. The result was an eighteen-page story entitled "Vergil's Home-coming," which contains in a nutshell the plot of the entire *Death of Vergil*. Immediately realizing that he had not done justice to the potentialities of the subject, Broch began writing a longer version, but he still thought that it could be mastered within the framework of an eighty-page novella—just as Thomas Mann, only a short time before, had originally conceived of his *Joseph* tetralogy as a brief narrative.

At this point a second impetus was added. In 1938, after the *Anschluss*, Broch was arrested by the Gestapo. During his five months in prison he came face to face with the imminence of death. He had hitherto been concerned theoretically with the problem of death; now he was confronted with its existential actuality. Whereas he had previously considered Vergil primarily as a prototype of the artist in a valueless society, he now devoted his attention to the *death* of Vergil. *"Vergil* was not written as a 'book,' but (under Hitler's threat) as my private discussion with death."

When he was released from prison, he managed with the aid of friends abroad (including Joyce, who had read Broch's essay on his work) to escape from Austria. After a few months in England and Scotland he came to the United States, where he arrived practically penniless in October of 1938. By 1940 the bulk of *Vergil* was finished, but Broch spent three more years—in New York and then in Princeton, where he settled down until 1949—polishing the manuscript. In 1945 the book was published simultaneously in English and German by the Pantheon Press in New York. The composition of the work is completely different from that of *The Sleepwalkers*, which was a pronounced case of additive composition and architectonic structuring. *The Death of Vergil* grew organically from within, by accretion and enrichment, from a novella of eighteen typed sheets to a printed work of more than five hundred pages.

The book depicts the last eighteen hours of Vergil's life—an obvious parallel to Joyce's work. Vergil arrives at the harbor of Brundisium on a September evening. He is borne through the reeking streets of the slums up to the palace of Augustus (Part One). After a fitful night (Part Two) in which he is beset by visions and self-recrimination at the waste of his own life, he spends his last morning (Part Three) talking with various friends. Just before he dies he gives in to Augustus's wish not to burn his manuscripts, but he elicits from the emperor, in return, the right to free his slaves. Then, in a final vision (Part Four), he glides gently into death.

Many readers have been perplexed, even dismayed, by the work. Aldous Huxley, in a letter to Broch, criticized the use of extensive philosophical lyricism with no contrasting passages of narrative:

My own feeling is that quantity destroys quality and that though, intrinsically, the sentences of which these sections are composed are rich with beauty and meaning, the very number of them—because of their intensity and their stylistic strangeness—imposes a strain upon the reader's mind and makes him, in the long run, incapable of reacting adequately to them.

Many readers, even the most sympathetic, would probably agree with Huxley. The effect of the work is like reading a five-hundred-page psalm: there is the same mixture of rhapsodic fervor, erotic imagery, and hymnic effusion. Only the third section is frankly narrative: it consists largely of conversations between Vergil and various visitors, including the dramatic high point of the work: the confrontation with Emperor Augustus. The long second section, on the other hand, is totally lyrical, unrelieved by any narrative, with disembodied imagery that remains frustratingly intangible.

Part of the difficulty in dealing with this work lies in the fact that Broch was consciously striving to create a new genre; to treat it as a novel is to criticize it unfairly. Alone among Broch's major prose works it does not bear the designation "novel." In his letters and essays Broch consistently referred to it as a lyrical work. He observed that the book is "a poem, though not in the sense of a single lyrical outburst and also not in the sense of a poem cycle on a central theme; yet a poem and, moreover, one that extends in a single breath over more than five hundred pages." The book is thus a novel only in the broad sense of German Romantic writers like Friedrich

Schlegel, for whom the novel was "progressive" and "universal," embracing all poetic forms. To understand this is not to accept the method uncritically. Broch forgets that lyric poetry is effective precisely because it concentrates into a highly compressed distillate the emotion that evaporates when spread out over hundreds of pages. Few readers, if any, are capable of reading through the second part without bogging down and thus losing the intended lyrical impact.

Despite this central criticism the book is one of the major literary works of the century; the conception alone is a daring step forward in the realm of poetry. Broch is concerned again with the resolution of the antinomies of life. From the very first page we are struck by a barrage of contrasts: above and below, within and without, here and beyond, past and present, motion and rest, I and All. Especially in the first half of the novel, life is presented as completely fragmented; nothing is whole. Vergil becomes increasingly aware of the dissonances of life and of the necessity to resolve them in order to attain any semblance of harmony. In *The Sleepwalkers* Broch presented this breakdown through disintegration of style, descending from the lyricism of the narrative poem to the rationality of the essay. Here he wishes to do more than depict fragmented reality; he wants to show the resolution of it all—in Vergil's mind as well as stylistically. Resolution is possible only when all aspects of reality can be brought together in a simultaneous vision: past, present, and future as well as life and death. A resolution of this sort can be accomplished only in sentences of a grand scope, and so Broch conceived as the underlying pattern of his book the idea: "one thought, one moment, one sentence." This almost monomaniacal consistency produced some of the longest sentences ever written in the German langauge—sentences beside which even the more adventurous efforts of Thomas Mann pale. "One can probably claim," Broch wrote proudly, "that the sentences in the adagio of the second part belong to the longest in world literature." Broch justified this by his assumption that only a poetic form is "capable of producing unity of the disparate and making it plausible, for in a poem the utterance does not fulfill itself in the rational expression, but in the irrational tension between the words, between the lines, in short: in the 'architecture of meaning.'"

Broch buttressed this "architecture of meaning" in various ways. Each of the four sections has a central symbol (water, fire, earth, and ether) as well as a basic mood, which Broch conceived in musical terms (*andante, adagio,* [no specific term], *maestoso*). The repetition and development of the various motives is treated consciously as musical variation. Broch's essay "Remarks on the Death of Vergil" indicates to what an incredible extent even the slightest details of the work have been plotted to intensify the "architecture of meaning." In German literature there is no other prose work besides Rilke's *The Notebooks of Malte Laurids Brigge* that must be read with the same attention and intensity as one reads a poem.

Within this "symphonic" framework the book has a distinct rhythm of development. In "The Arrival" Vergil is shocked into an awareness of the disjointedness of life. In his feverish state he is keenly aware of polarities: the leisure on board the ship and the agonies of the slaves groaning over the oars below; the blue sky above and the dark waters below; the stench and poverty of the slums and the luxury of Augustus's lofty palace. That night, as these impressions unite with memory in his feverish vision ("The Descent"), he comes to the frightful realization that his entire life as well as his work have excluded an entire half of existence; he has willfully shut out grief and ugliness for the sake of beauty alone. What the first part presented in visual contrasts and the second part in a lyrical inner vision, the third part ("The Expectation") re-capitulates in dialectical arguments between Vergil and his friends. In "The Home-coming," finally, all of these conflicting elements are resolved in a grand vision of unity as Vergil dies.

Vergil arrives at three important turning points during these last hours. The first comes during the night, in Part Two, when he decides, as a gesture of expiation, to burn *The Aeneid*. In Vergil's mind his masterpiece has become a symbol of his own imperfection. For just as he had carefully filtered all disturbances out of his own life, so too had he distilled the reality of his poem until there was nothing left but beauty. *The Aeneid* is thus a living memorial to his "perjury" of reality, and he feels that he can atone for his guilt only by consigning his work to destruction.

The second turning point comes at the end of his audience with Emperor Augustus, a brilliant exercise in dialectics between the representatives of two cultural epochs. Augustus is an idealized totalitarian; for him all life revolves around the state, and the individual finds meaning only through service to the state. Vergil, on the other hand, is what Broch called a pre-Christian—he has his foot all but on the threshold of a new system of Christian values in which a concern for the individual will outweigh the totalitarian concept of imperial Rome. Because neither of these strong-willed men can understand the other, the dialogue does not become real communication, but merely a statement of position in which they talk past each other. It illustrates the dilemma of "no longer and not yet," for Augustus represents an age that is virtually past while Vergil speaks with the voice of an era that has not yet come. (Actually the theme of "no longer and not yet" has been subtly altered in this novel to "no longer and yet already" because Vergil has such strong premonitions of the future.) Vergil

[35]

tries to explain his decision to destroy *The Aeneid*, but Augustus objects that the poet has fulfilled his ethical responsibility by creating a symbol of the state in all its glory. He is of course offended when Vergil insists that the present Roman state is in itself no longer real, but merely the symbol of a human reality that still lies in the future: the Christian world. At this point the story takes an unexpected twist that betrays the *novella* origin of the plot. The two men have grown increasingly heated in the defense of their respective positions and the argument becomes quite personal. Suddenly Vergil, relenting almost without motivation, agrees to give Augustus the manuscript. He has perceived—Broch implies this rather than states it—that it calls for an even greater sacrifice to forgo his desire to burn the manuscript. By destroying his poetry he would merely have gained a passing satisfaction; it would be a gesture of defiance. But by renouncing this wish he is able to commit an act of human love, thus anticipating in his own way the era of human commitment which is to come.

The third turning point comes at the end of the fourth part. Vergil's death, though lyrical in tone, is not abstract, disembodied, or intangible. It is related at each step to a great mystical vision that derives its imagery from the story of the creation—but a creation experienced in reverse. Step by step, as he sinks out of life, Vergil feels himself moving progressively back through earlier stages of being: back through Paradise; back through the stages of animal, plant, and mineral life; back through the original separation of light and dark to the source of all being. And at that point—two pages from the end of the book—reunited with God, he turns around, and in one final vision, surveys all of life and reality. From this new position of reunification with the All he can now see the pattern of wholeness in life. All the polarities have disappeared. In Death all opposites are reconciled. Life and Death become one and the same. It is a conjuration of the *coincidentia oppositorum* that is unmatched in literature, probably, since the ecstatic visions of fourteenth-century mystics like Meister Eckhart. (Certainly its only modern counterpart is to be found in Novalis's lovely and mysterious *Hymns to the Night*.) In the hymnic prose of the finale this ending is plausible and stirring. Where the second part of the book failed in its cerebral and spiritualized lyricism, this section captures the imagination through its tactile vividness and carries the reader along with Vergil into the final vision of unity. Here, where the contradictions outlined in the first part are recapitulated and resolved, the reader feels that the long road has been worth while. The effect is that of an intense lyric poem, but a poem escalated into cosmic dimensions. This final section, which represents the *terminus ad quem* of the preceding five hundred pages, is one of the most powerful passages in modern literature.

The representation of death and dying, in which the work culminates, is more than a gesture of literary virtuosity. It fulfills an important function in Broch's development, paving the way for future thought. If we live in fear of death, then we cannot free our minds for the ethical problems of life. Broch wanted, by bringing death into his life and work, to annul its threat and thus open the way to an ethical system based not upon fear of death but purely upon the demands of life. In *The Unknown Quantity* death functioned as no more than the manifestation of the irrational "irruption from below." Mother Gisson, in *The Bewitchment*, had achieved a "knowledge of the heart" in which life and death are one; but Broch portrayed her from the outside, as an ideal, through the not unbiased eyes of the doctor, and the reader must accept her spiritual harmony as an article of faith. In *Vergil* Broch wanted actually to create the experience of death—and

[37]

to allow the reader to share in it—as an extension of life rather than as chaos and nothingness. This is the meaning of the fourth part, in which Vergil moves toward death through a series of transformations showing that death is the source and complement of life—that it is merely another form of life. In this way death constitutes a resolution of the introductory opposites, for grief and agony, sickness and misery are elongations of death protruding into life, just as death is an extension of life into another realm—another typically Romantic attitude that Broch shares with contemporaries like Rilke and Hermann Hesse. When Vergil comes to terms with death, he likewise resolves the dissonant elements of the earlier passages by accepting them as an inevitable complement to life. Now that death—and its various extensions—no longer constitutes a threat, Broch can devote himself to a purely existential analysis of life in this world.

Broch considered that he had "finished [his] literary career once and for all" with *The Death of Vergil*. During the last ten years of his life he regarded his occasional literary work as a distinct and unpleasant intrusion upon more important undertakings. Throughout Broch's life we can observe an absolute consistency of thought and action. In *Vergil* he reached the conclusion that ethical action was the responsibility of the individual. Since he saw a possibility for "concretization of ethics" only in politics, he devoted most of his energies to political theory and practical service. As a matter of fact, his literary work is almost totally confined to the brief period from 1928 to 1940; even his last novel, completed in 1949–50, is based on stories written during the thirties. During and after the war Broch was indefatigable in his efforts to help refugees, and from his meager resources, to send CARE packages to needy friends in Europe. His "absolute incapacity to hurt anyone" prompted him to spend hours answering letters—often as many as two hundred and fifty a month. During the last five years of his life he frequently spoke almost mystically of the "seven projects" that he had in hand, and he was fond of comparing himself to Kafka's "Country Doctor," who, drive as hard as he may, can never reach the next village. Broch was a dynamo of energy, capable of working intensively for eighteen hours a day. As he felt himself growing older this natural energy was intensified by what he called his "panic of not finishing." This "panic" was surely not lessened by the fact that he had no steady means of support. He was particularly anxious to complete his three-volume study of mass psychology because he hoped, on its merits, to obtain a professorship at Princeton that would afford him some measure of financial security. (He turned down a position at the East German University of Jena.) Meanwhile he lived at the expense of various foundations—Guggenheim, Rockefeller, Bollingen, Oberlaender, The American Academy of Arts and Letters—and from the income of occasional commissioned "literary" projects, such as the study of Hofmannsthal. In 1949 Broch moved from Princeton to New Haven, where efforts were in progress to obtain for him an honorary professorship in the German Department at Yale University. He was on the point of returning to Europe for the first time since his emigration when a heart attack abruptly ended his life in 1951. At the time of his death various groups in the United States and Austria were proposing him for the Nobel Prize, an honor he would doubtless have received had he lived a few years longer. Broch is buried in Killingworth, Connecticut—a strange resting place for a man whose intense sincerity alone prevented him from becoming a caricature of the European intellectual.

Broch's last novel, prompted by financial needs, had grown from humble beginnings to significant proportions—a pattern we have repeatedly observed. In 1949 Broch received the proofs of five early stories that his publisher wished to reprint as a book in order to profit from the *succès d'estime* that Broch had won with *The Death of Vergil*. As Broch read through the stories, he became aware both of their insufficiencies and of the common theme that seemed to run through all of them. He decided to supplement the old stories with a few new ones, put them into a framework, and publish them as a "novel in eleven stories"—*The Innocents*. The result, an indictment of the political indifference that led to the rise of National Socialism, is a direct offshoot of Broch's political theories. He explained his intentions in an epilogue:

The novel portrays German conditions and types of the pre-Hitler period. The figures chosen for this purpose are completely "unpolitical"; inasmuch as they have any political ideas at all, they hover in a vague and foggy realm. None of them is directly "guilty" for the Hitler catastrophe. For that reason the book is called "The Innocents." Yet precisely this is the intellectual and emotional atmosphere from which . . . Nazism won its real powers. Political indifference is ethical indifference and hence, in the last analysis, closely related to ethical perversion. In short, the politically "innocent" are already situated rather deep in the realm of ethical guilt.

Like *The Sleepwalkers* it is architectonically structured, spanning the full gamut of styles from lyricism to essayism. The novel is introduced by a parable in the form of Martin Buber's Hasidic tales—a fact not without interest since the theme of engagement between the I and the Thou is reminiscent of Buber's philosophy. The narrative consists of three groups of stories that take place in 1913, 1923, and 1933; each cycle is introduced by a "Canto" (not unlike Brecht's ballads in their style) that represents the "voice" of the era.

The central figure is the young Dutch merchant Andreas, a man who has spent his life fleeing every sort of commitment.

Because of his "fear of exams" he originally left school and home, emigrating to South Africa. This "fear of exams" is the symbolic motive of his existence. Whenever a situation arose in which he was compelled to make a decision, he simply moved on. As a result of his ready adaptability—like Huguenau—he accumulated a fortune in diamonds. He is a man, neither good nor bad, completely without attachments in life. When we first catch a glimpse of him in a Paris café in 1913 he has just lost his mother. Ten years later, in Germany, Andreas is seeking the comforts of home and love without being willing to commit himself in return. He rents a room in the home of an elderly baroness and gradually manages to insinuate his way into her affections as the son of the house. At the same time he engages in a love affair with a young girl, Melitta. Hildegard, the baroness's daughter, regards the two acts as irreconcilable. If Andreas has forced his way into two different sets of lives, then he must face the consequences and commit himself to one or the other. He has won the confidence of the baroness as well as Melitta. One or the other must be hurt, ultimately, when he breaks off the relationship. Hildegard urges Andreas to make up his mind; finally she takes action herself. She tells Melitta that Andreas is going to marry her, Hildegard; Melitta commits suicide. That same night Hildegard invites Andreas into her bedroom, and in one of the weirdest love scenes of literature, deliberately makes him impotent so that he will never again be tempted to desert her mother or make another girl unhappy. Ten years later, when Andreas is comfortably established with the baroness, Melitta's grandfather finds him. In their conversation Andreas becomes aware of his great guilt. Until now he had regarded Hildegard as Melitta's murderess; now he sees that it was his own lack of moral responsibility that really caused her death, and he commits suicide. This is the skeletal plot of the stories.

As usual Broch has filled out the very slight plot with symbolic elements that bear the burden of meaning. We have already spoken of the triangle, which occurs unobtrusively in many of the stories as a symbol of the artificially isolated existence that tries to shield itself from commitment to reality. Then, the entire novel is based loosely on the legend of Don Juan. Various of the names are borrowed from the legend (Andreas buys a house from a certain Herr von Juna); and many of the episodes correspond to the archetypal structure of the legend (the avenging grandfather comes to Andreas as a reincarnation of the stone guest). Further, the Andreas plot is paralleled by the contrasting story of the schoolmaster Zacharias. The two men represent opposite poles of human nature as indicated by their initials; Broch hopes to achieve symbolic totality by implying that their attitudes embrace the whole range of human behavior. Whereas Andreas represents ethical guilt out of total lack of commitment, Zacharias is the born follower, who commits himself blindly to a false system of values (Nazism). Their failure to respond to the actualities of existence is revealed, again, in sexual symbolism. Andreas's incompetence is signified by his ultimate impotence and suicide while Zacharias, an ideological tyrant in public, is beaten by his wife when he gets home at night. The only harmonious figure of the novel is the grandfather. As an authority on bee-keeping, he is closely linked to the powers of nature. Structurally his spirit permeates the entire novel since the "cantos" at the beginning of each section are ostensibly the songs that he sings, the conscience of his age.

On the one occasion when Andreas and Zacharias actually meet, they discuss Einstein's theory of relativity. Zacharias, the adherent of the closed system, rebels against the idea that reality is not hard and fast. As a teacher of mathematics he believes that he is justified, for pedagogic reasons, in ignoring new theories because they would confuse his pupils. In other words, he closes his eyes to any new conception of reality and follows a false prophet who promises to uphold the old order. Andreas, on the other hand, finds in the theory of relativity a perfect justification of his emotional lability and reluctance to take a stand. He allows himself to avoid the necessity of making decisions by saying that in a relativistic world all values are equally valid. It is only in his great confession, when the grandfather has convinced him of his guilt, that he admits: "I thought that I was fleeing irresponsibility, and in truth it was responsibility that I was fleeing. That is my guilt." In a world without absolutes, Andreas concludes, the proper human attitude cannot be attained "by a turn toward good, but only through a turning away from what is evil on earth. . . ." Because of his relativism he had failed to react against evil and thus had become guilty.

This last is not merely a piece of logical sophistry, but rather the result of Broch's most vital concern during his last years: his "Humane Politics." He had concluded that political absolutes, as expressed in the Bill of Rights, are just as invalid in our time as religious absolutes, because they too are founded upon the notion of inalienable transcendental rights of mankind. Broch pleaded instead for a supplement, which he called his Bill of Duties and which he submitted for consideration to the UN and other world organizations. We do not need to assume the existence of transcendental rights, Broch said. A whole system of ethics can be established upon the "earthly absolute" of total enslavement—the one act this side of death that deprives man of all human dignity. Assuming that total enslavement is the absolute evil, it is the responsibility of the individual—in fact, his duty—to rebel against any act that threatens to lead to enslavement of man in any form. In other words, since absolute good is unknown, we do not always know what we should act *for;* entire totalitarian systems have been justified by the claim that they are acting on behalf of the good of the people. But since we do know what is absolutely *evil* here on earth, it is our duty to rebel at any time against any threat to human freedom and dignity.

Broch has come a long way since *The Sleepwalkers,* for *The Innocents* is actually an indictment of purely "objective" men like Huguenau and passive followers like the villagers of Kuppron. *The Sleepwalkers* ended with the exhortation to brotherly love: "Do thyself no harm: for we are all here." In his Theory of Humane Politics Broch concluded that a positive affirmation of solidarity is not enough. It is man's duty to rebel "negatively" (his own term) against absolute evil on earth. This is the position of a man who has witnessed the horrors of totalitarianism and the concentration camp, which he came to regard as the modern symbol of absolute evil. This new ethical attitude explains his efforts to reshape the political thought of the postwar world by supplementing the conception of human "rights" with a bill of human "duties."

It is one of life's ironies that Broch, who struggled against "literature" most of his life, will always be known primarily as a novelist. The work he most prided himself on—his theory of values, epistemology, philosophy of history, mass psychology, and political theory—either remained virtually unknown or found no more than indirect expression in his novels. Attempts to present Broch as a systematic philosopher are probably futile. His own "impatience for cognition" prevented him from evolving any real system, and his total commitment to life engendered a dynamic development rather than any static and formalized attitude. His "philosophy" is to be found as much in his life, letters, and fiction as in his philosophical essays. In the last analysis, moreover, his ideas were not so original as he thought. To be sure, he formulated his own unique synthesis and coined brilliant phrases that appeal to the mind. But the elements of his thought, if not derivative of Kant's critical idealism and Hegel's dialectics, often parallel the existential analysis of thinkers like Jaspers or Camus. This is not to denigrate the substance of Broch's thought. There is nobility in his conception of man's freedom, dignity and responsibility, just as there is dignity in the pattern of his life. But his real contribution is literary. Whereas one of his ideas often summons up associations with many other thinkers of the past and present, a page of his prose is instantly recognizable as his alone.

Broch never made his works easy for the reader. He once wrote that Joyce's weakness was his uncompromising attitude, but the second part of *The Death of Vergil* is just as thorny as *Finnegans Wake*, without the compensation of Joyce's wit and sense of realism. On the other hand, Broch never made life or writing easy for himself. He was conscious of a mission in life, to which he devoted himself with absolute consistency and an almost messianic zeal. Yet the reader who is willing to follow Broch into the mazes of his works—whether the analytic landscape of *The Sleepwalkers* or the luxuriant jungle of *The Death of Vergil*—and to succumb to the curious synthesis of rationalism and mysticism, will come away enriched by a new dimension. Broch's vision of the immanence of death will probably be regarded as his most original contribution to human experience. His evocation of the totality and simultaneity of life is his greatest achievement in literature.

SELECTED BIBLIOGRAPHY

NOTE: *Most of Broch's manuscripts, including much unpublished literary and biographical material, are deposited in the Germanics Collection of the Yale University Library. I have quoted from the following items: a methodological prospectus entitled "Der Roman 'Die Schlafwandler' " (written in 1930 for a publisher); English synopsis of "The Bewitchment" (written for the Guggenheim Foundation, around 1940).*

The standard edition of Broch's collected works, with valuable introductions, is published by the Rhein-Verlag in Zürich.

PRINCIPAL WORKS OF HERMANN BROCH

Vol. 1. Gedichte. Edited by Erich Kahler. 1953.

Vol. 2. Die Schlafwandler. Eine Romantrilogie. 1952. (First edition: 1931–32.)

Vol. 3. Der Tod des Vergil. 1952. (First edition: New York, Pantheon, 1945.)

Vol. 4. Der Versucher. Roman. Edited by Felix Stössinger. 1953.

Vol. 5. Die Schuldlosen. Roman in elf Erzählungen. Edited by Hermann Weigand. 1954. (First edition: München, Weismann, 1950.)

Vol. 6. Dichten und Erkennen. (Essays I.) Edited by Hannah Arendt. 1955.

Vol. 7. Erkennen und Handeln. (Essays II.) Edited by Hannah Arendt. 1955.

Vol. 8. Briefe. Von 1929 bis 1951. Edited by Robert Pick. 1957.

Vol. 9. Massenpsychologie. Schriften aus dem Nachlass. Edited by Wolfgang Rothe. 1959.

Vol. 10. Die unbekannte Grösse und frühe Schriften. Edited by Ernst Schönwiese. 1961. (First serialized in *Vossische Zeitung*, 1933.)

Translations of Broch's Works

The Sleepwalkers. A Trilogy. Translated by Willa and Edwin Muir. Boston, Little, Brown, 1932. 2nd edition: New York, Pantheon, 1947; reissued 1964.

The Unknown Quantity. Translated by Willa and Edwin Muir. New York, Viking Press, 1935.

The Death of Virgil. Translated by Jean Starr Untermeyer. New York, Pantheon, 1945.

Arendt, Hannah. "The Achievement of Hermann Broch," *Kenyon Review*, XI (1949), 476–83.

Blanchot, Maurice. Le livre à venir. Paris, Gallimard, 1959.

Blöcker, Günter. Die neuen Wirklichkeiten. Berlin, Argon Verlag, 1957, pp. 307–18.

Brinkmann, Richard. "Romanform und Werttheorie bei Hermann Broch: Strukturprobleme moderner Dichtung," *Deutsche Vierteljahrsschrift für Literaturwissenschaft und Geistesgeschichte*, XXXI (1957), 169–97.

Cassirer, Sidonie. "Hermann Broch's Early Writings," *Publications of the Modern Language Association*, LXXV (1960), 453–62.

Faber du Faur, Curt von. "Der Seelenführer in Hermann Brochs Tod des Vergil," in Wächter und Hüter (Festschrift für Hermann J. Weigand). New Haven, Yale University Dept. of Germanic Languages, 1957, pp. 147–61.

Geissler, Rolf. Möglichkeiten des modernen deutschen Romans. Frankfurt am Main, Berlin, Bonn, Moritz Diesterweg, 1962, pp. 102–60.

Herd, Eric W. "Hermann Broch and the Legitimacy of the Novel," *German Life and Letters*, XIII (1960), 262–77.

Jens, Walter. Statt einer Literaturgeschichte. Pfullingen, Neske, 1957, pp. 109–31.

Jonas, Klaus W. "Hermann Broch. Eine bibliographische Studie" (compiled with the collaboration of Lothar E. Zeidler), *Philobiblon*, VI (1962), 291–323.

Kahler, Erich. Die Philosophie von Hermann Broch. Tübingen, Mohr, 1962.

────── ed. Dichter wider Willen. Einführung in das Werk von Hermann Broch. Zürich, Rhein-Verlag, 1958. (Contains contributions by Wilhelm Alt, Hannah Arendt, Karl August Horst, Erich Kahler, Thilo Koch, and Heinz Politzer.)

Mandelkow, Karl Robert. Hermann Brochs Romantrilogie Die Schlafwandler. Gestaltung und Reflexion im modernen deutschen Roman. Heidelberg, C. Winter, 1962.

Martini, Fritz. Das Wagnis der Sprache. Stuttgart, Ernst Klett, 1954, pp. 413–64.

Rothe, Wolfgang. "Der junge Broch," *Neue deutsche Hefte*, VII (1960), 780–97.

Schoolfield, George C. "Notes on Hermann Broch's Der Versucher," *Monatshefte für deutschen Unterricht*, XLVIII (1956), 1–16.

———— "Broch's Sleepwalkers: Aeneas and the Apostles," *James Joyce Review*, II (1958), 21–38.

Stössinger, Felix. "Hermann Broch," in Deutsche Literatur im 20. Jahrhundert. Edited by Hermann Friedmann and Otto Mann. Heidelberg, Rothe, 1956, pp. 345–61.

Strelka, Joseph. Kafka, Musil, Broch und die Entwicklung des modernen Romans. Wien, Forum, 1959.

Weigand, Hermann J. "Broch's Death of Vergil: Program Notes," *Publications of the Modern Language Association*, LXII (1947), 525–54.

———— "Hermann Broch's Die Schuldlosen: An Approach," *Publications of the Modern Language Association*, LXVIII (1953), 323–34.

"A Writer's Conscience," *Times Literary Supplement*, March 29, 1963, pp. 209–10.

Ziolkowski, Theodore. "Zur Entstehung und Struktur von Hermann Brochs Schlafwandlern," *Deutsche Vierteljahrsschrift für Literaturwissenschaft und Geistesgeschichte*, XXXVIII (1964), 40–69.